Excel Simplified

How to use Excel at ease

Yosef Andreas

Excel Simplified

Yosef Andreas

INTRODUCTION

I used to think that Excel is a complex program. However, I have to use this program every single day, since my job demands me to analyze bunch of data. A lot of data – actually. As I learned and used Excel regularly, I found that it can offer many ways to solve a problem, and for me: the simpler the better. This is where Excel start to gain my attention. As long as I can find a simplified way to solve the complex problem in the less time, I'll be more than satisfied.

This book will not cover the entire Excel area. I only focus on how to enjoy doing work with Excel, especially tips for:

- Keyboard Shortcuts
- Conditional Formatting
- Filtering
- VLOOKUP
- Charting
- VBA
- Other helpful tips

I am not an Excel expert or even Microsoft MVP. However, I found that the tips I share in this book has helped me conquering my daily task with ease and impress my co-workers or boss. I hope this will help you, too.

Happy simplifying.
Yosef Andreas

KEYBOARD SHORTCUTS

"The best route to access flawless action"

In Excel, the less you use the mouse, the quicker you complete the task. This is where keyboard shortcuts make their role. Below are the helpful keyboard shortcuts that worth to remember – they really save your time.

Ctrl+S

If you do not want to lose your work, this shortcut will save your life.

Ctrl+Z

Don't be afraid to make mistake. You can undo it anytime you want.

Ctrl+1

You can use it to format anything: be it a cell, chart, shape or text box. Hitting this button will activate the formatting dialog box

F2

Do you want to edit the cell without moving your mouse to the formula bar or double-clicking the cell? Just press F2 – as simple as that.

F4

There are two ways to use this shortcut:

- Repeat last performed action.
- Toggle for changing cell reference style to relative or absolute (only works while in formula editing)

Ctrl+Page Up

Switch to previous sheet

Ctrl+Page Down

Switch to next sheet

Ctrl+F6

So many workbook being opened and you want to switch at ease? Use this shortcut.

Ctrl+Arrow

Jump to the end direction accordingly, very handy for navigating around the workbook

Ctrl+Shift+Arrow

Select the entire direction accordingly.

Ctrl+* (on the numpad)

Select the entire region

Ctrl+F3

Open the Name Manager

F3

Use this key to paste the named ranges into the formula

Alt

By hitting this single keyboard button will display the Letter of any menu, just type the respective letter to activate each menu.

Ctrl+Enter

You can use this to fill different cell with the same value or formula. If you use it on the single cell, you can enter the cell's content and keep the cell selected.

Ctrl+R

When you are in case of copying the formula to next column, Ctrl+R is all you need. Just select the column together with the cell containing the original formula and then hit that shortcut.

Ctrl+D

This shortcut has the same principle with the Ctrl+R, except that Excel will copy it down instead of right.

Conditional Formatting

"You can define your own formatting style"

Conditional Formatting (also known as CF) is a tool that allows you to apply formats to a cell or range of cells, and have that formatting change depending on the value of the cells or the value of a formula.

Define when your schedule is due or overdue

Assume that you have a list containing a task with the timeline like shown in Figure and you want to get the quick insight whether the task is due or overdue. With conditional formatting and TODAY function, you can make it dynamic as it updates itself whenever you open the workbook.

	A	B	C	D
1				
2			**Task List**	
3				
4		Last Update		11/29/2015
5		**No**	**Name**	**Timeline**
6		1	Task 1	11/29/2015
7		2	Task 2	11/30/2015
8		3	Task 3	10/21/2015
9		4	Task 4	12/13/2015
10		5	Task 5	9/23/2015
11		6	Task 6	11/22/2015
12		7	Task 7	12/24/2015
13		8	Task 8	12/28/2015
14		9	Task 9	11/20/2015
15		10	Task 10	11/28/2015

In the cell D4, type =TODAY() in the formula box. This function returns to current date according to your computer clock. Then select the timeline value (i.e. cell D6:D15) then go to conditional formatting and select rule to format only cells that less than or equal to cell D4. In this case, I set the formatting to bold, red font color and fill the cell with yellow.

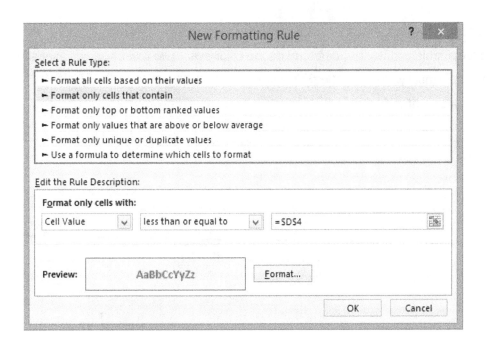

Now you can easily track the timeline that is due or overdue. The coolest part of this trick is the list will be updated whenever you open the workbook since cell D4 contains the TODAY function.

	A	B	C	D
1				
2			**Task List**	
3				
4			Last Update	11/29/2015
5		**No**	**Name**	**Timeline**
6		1	Task 1	11/29/2015
7		2	Task 2	11/30/2015
8		3	Task 3	10/21/2015
9		4	Task 4	12/13/2015
10		5	Task 5	9/23/2015
11		6	Task 6	11/22/2015
12		7	Task 7	12/24/2015
13		8	Task 8	12/28/2015
14		9	Task 9	11/20/2015
15		10	Task 10	11/28/2015

Create a Shading Rows

If you have a large table and want to differentiate the color every two rows, use conditional formatting instead of doing it manually. Here are the simple steps:

Select the range you want to format

	Name	Target	Actual	Progress
	Project 1	100,00%	50,00%	IN PROGRESS
	Project 2	100,00%	60,00%	IN PROGRESS
	Project 3	100,00%	80,00%	IN PROGRESS
	Project 4	100,00%	100,00%	DONE
	Project 5	100,00%	70,00%	IN PROGRESS
	Project 6	100,00%	90,00%	IN PROGRESS
	Project 7	100,00%	100,00%	DONE
	Project 8	100,00%	100,00%	DONE
	Project 9	100,00%	50,00%	IN PROGRESS
	Project 10	100,00%	40,00%	IN PROGRESS

Go into the conditional formatting menu, and then select "Use a formula to determine which cells to format" on the New Formatting Rule:

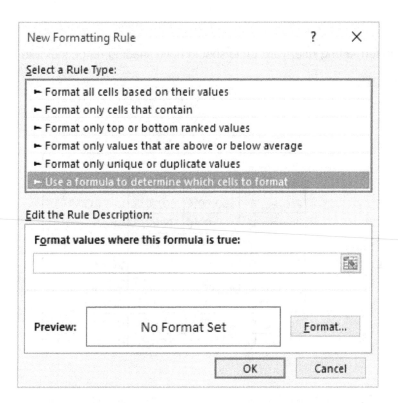

In the text box, type formula =MOD(ROW();2) and then format the cell fill with the color as you want:

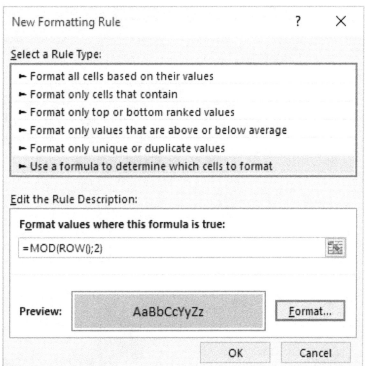

Click OK and apply the formatting rule, your table should have shading range look like below:

	Name	Target	Actual	Progress
	Project 1	100,00%	50,00%	IN PROGRESS
	Project 2	100,00%	60,00%	IN PROGRESS
	Project 3	100,00%	80,00%	IN PROGRESS
	Project 4	100,00%	100,00%	DONE
	Project 5	100,00%	70,00%	IN PROGRESS
	Project 6	100,00%	90,00%	IN PROGRESS
	Project 7	100,00%	100,00%	DONE
	Project 8	100,00%	100,00%	DONE
	Project 9	100,00%	50,00%	IN PROGRESS
	Project 10	100,00%	40,00%	IN PROGRESS

The benefit of applying this formatting is that the shading range automatically adjusted each time you insert or delete the row between the ranges.

Display Value as Data Bar

Conditional Formatting can be used to display cell value as data bar. This is very useful when you want your progress report to be displayed with clarity. The trick is very simple though, and we will use the table below as example:

	A	B	C	D
1				
2			**Project Name**	**Progess**
3			Project A	60%
4			Project B	70%
5			Project C	40%
6			Project D	50%
7			Project E	20%
8			Project F	80%

The table is simple and you already know which project is nearly complete or just started by looking the value. With conditional formatting, you will have better than that. Select the entire progress value, go to Conditional Formatting menu, and select the first option (Format all cells based on their values) in the rule type. Choose **data bar** as format style and hit OK. Your table will be like below:

	A	B	C	D
1				
2			**Project Name**	**Progess**
3			Project A	60%
4			Project B	70%
5			Project C	40%
6			Project D	50%
7			Project E	20%
8			Project F	80%

To get a clearer look, I adjust the width of column D and format the number with white font at the left alignment, or if you prefer, you can tick the **Show Bar Only** in the formatting rule.

Project Name	Progess
Project A	60%
Project B	70%
Project C	40%
Project D	50%
Project E	20%
Project F	80%

Comparing data without any help of chart

These tips are quite simple yet effective, especially if you want to present data of comparison without using the chart. For the example, look at the data below:

Project Name	Progress	
	Mr. X	Mr. Y
Project A	75%	80%
Project B	30%	30%
Project C	50%	45%
Project D	89%	75%
Project E	45%	60%
Project F	90%	70%

To make the data more digested, we'll be using the same technique of displaying value as data bar, but the bar direction of Mr. X will be opposite to Mr. Y. In the formatting rule for Mr. X, select the Bar Direction to Right-to-left. The data is now easier to read, isn't it?

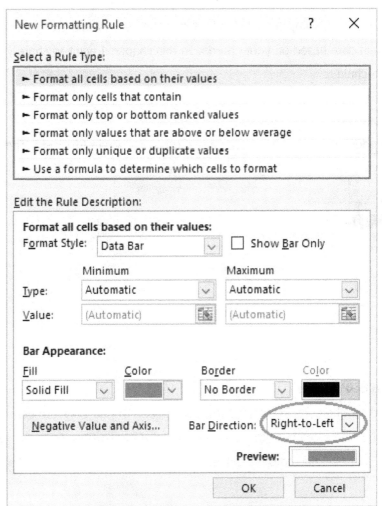

Project Name	Progress	
	Mr. X	Mr. Y
Project A	75%	80%
Project B	30%	30%
Project C	50%	45%
Project D	89%	75%
Project E	45%	60%
Project F	90%	70%

Filtering

"You only see what you need"

Filter for data in Excel is a simple implementation that can handle very complex criteria expressions. It can help you view certain data based on your criteria. In this chapter I want to share you some simple-to-implement filtering technique.

Activate the filter Instantly

Select the column headers you want to filter, and then press **Ctrl+Shift+L**. The filter tools are indicated by a dropdown triangle on the right side of the cell.

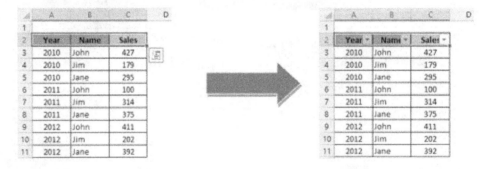

Quick Filtering using cell's value

We are going to use data above to implement this technique. To see only the John records, simply right-click any cell in the Name column that represents John. Choose filter from the resulting context menu and then select Filter by Selected Cell's Value.

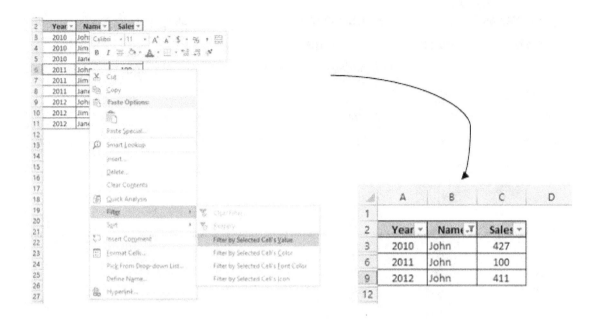

Introducing Table

To make managing and analyzing groups of related data easier, you can transform the range of cells into Excel Table (previously known as Excel List for Microsoft Excel 2003). To transform your data into the table, select the data and then press **Ctrl+T**. Excel Table has so many features that manages inside its rows and columns easier. It includes:

1. Built Filtering and Sorting on Header Row – it is enabled on every header row so that you can filter or sort the data quickly.

Product	Quarter 1	Quarter 2	Quarter 3	Quarter 4	Grand Total
Apple	$600.00	$823.00	$978.00	$473.00	
Orange	$364.00	$879.00	$743.00	$574.00	
Grape	$543.00	$683.00	$372.00	$423.00	
Strawberry	$550.00	$763.00	$368.00	$1,000.00	
Pineapple	$631.00	$580.00	$384.00	$769.00	
Melon	$505.00	$663.00	$437.00	$536.00	

2. Banded rows – your data automatically formatted as table by default, giving it the table style with banded rows.

3. Multiple tables as you want – unlike usual data filtering which only allow you to create one data filtering in one sheet, you can create table as many as you want

4. Dynamic cell ranges – any new data added to the table will automatically update the formula or chart referring it.

5. Column headers in formula – any column header in the table can be assigned in the formula. To use it, type the open bracket symbol ([) to display the column header list. Select it using mouse or keyboard and then press Tab key to use it into the formula.

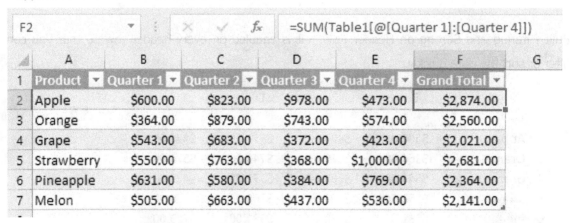

6. Calculated columns – By entering a formula in one cell in a table column, that formula is instantly applied to all other cells in that table column.

	A	B	C	D	E	F	G
	F2				f_x	=SUM(Table1[@[Quarter 1]:[Quarter 4]])	
1	Product	Quarter 1	Quarter 2	Quarter 3	Quarter 4	Grand Total	
2	Apple	$600.00	$823.00	$978.00	$473.00	$2,874.00	
3	Orange	$364.00	$879.00	$743.00	$574.00	$2,560.00	
4	Grape	$543.00	$683.00	$372.00	$423.00	$2,021.00	
5	Strawberry	$550.00	$763.00	$368.00	$1,000.00	$2,681.00	
6	Pineapple	$631.00	$580.00	$384.00	$769.00	$2,364.00	
7	Melon	$505.00	$663.00	$437.00	$536.00	$2,141.00	

7. Automatic size expansion – you can add new data to the bottom of the table and Excel will recognize it as a part of the table.

8. Tab key to add new row – simply press it in the lower right of your table.

9. Sizing handle – besides Tab key, you can use sizing handle in the lower-right corner of the table that allows you to drag the table to the size that you want.

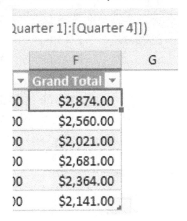

10. Total row - You can add a total row to your table that provides access to summary functions (such as the AVERAGE, or SUM function). To do this, select the table, go to Table tools and then check the Total Row at Table Style Options.

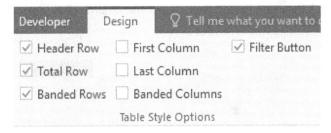

A drop-down list appears in each total row cell so that you can quickly calculate the totals that you want.

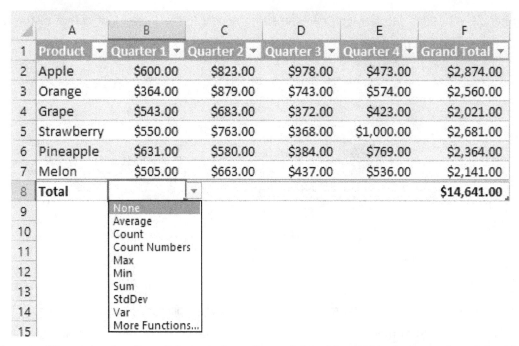

	A	B	C	D	E	F
1	Product ▼	Quarter 1 ▼	Quarter 2 ▼	Quarter 3 ▼	Quarter 4 ▼	Grand Total ▼
2	Apple	$600.00	$823.00	$978.00	$473.00	$2,874.00
3	Orange	$364.00	$879.00	$743.00	$574.00	$2,560.00
4	Grape	$543.00	$683.00	$372.00	$423.00	$2,021.00
5	Strawberry	$550.00	$763.00	$368.00	$1,000.00	$2,681.00
6	Pineapple	$631.00	$580.00	$384.00	$769.00	$2,364.00
7	Melon	$505.00	$663.00	$437.00	$536.00	$2,141.00
8	Total	▼				$14,641.00
9		None				
10		Average				
11		Count				
		Count Numbers				
12		Max				
13		Min				
		Sum				
14		StdDev				
		Var				
15		More Functions...				

11. Slicer to filter data visually – this tools is really useful to filter Table faster and easier with single click. To insert slicer, click insert slicer and then select the column that you want to filter.

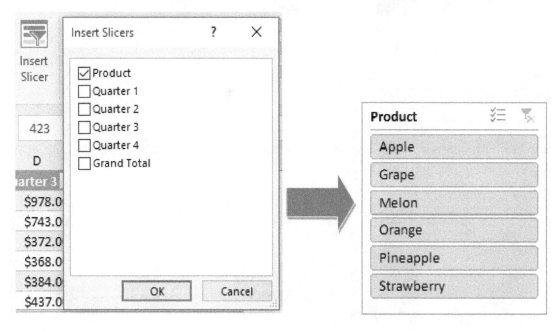

VLOOKUP

"Look up vertically and retrieve"

VLOOKUP (stands for vertical lookup) is really handy for helping you retrieve the data / information from a bunch (or huge) range, according to the value in the leftmost column of the table. The function has four arguments as follow:

VLOOKUP(**lookup_value**; table_array; col_index_num; [range_lookup])

Which translates into:

"Lookup this value (**lookup_value**), into that range (**table_array**), at the nth column (**col_index_num**), based on matching criteria (**range_lookup**, either TRUE (1) for approximate match or FALSE (0) for exact match)"

To completely understand how the function works, let's see the example below:

	A	B	C
	#ID	Name	Status
1	2001	John	Active
2	2002	Jim	Inactive
3	2003	Jane	Active
4	2004	Jeff	Inactive
5	2005	Jack	Active
6	2006	Jessica	Inactive
7	2007	Jude	Active
8	2008	Johnson	Active
9	2009	Julian	Inactive
10	2010	Jackie	Active

I have a table of employment data consisting three columns, which represent employee ID, Name, and Employment Status. We can find the information about name or status by looking the ID number with the help of VLOOKUP. I name the range A2:C11 with employment. Since the name is in the second column, we will use 2 as col_index_num argument thus the formula will become like this:

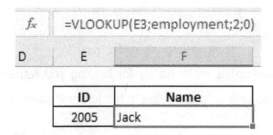

And the result is Jack. Using the same formula, we want to know his employment status. So, change the col_index_num to 3

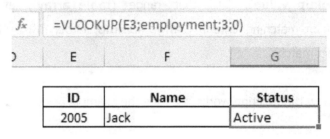

As you can see, I tend to use 1 or 0 than TRUE or FALSE for range_lookup argument. This way I can maintain my formula as simplified as possible.

VLOOKUP with MATCH Combo

Previously, we used number in the column index number. The problem with this way is that the formula will be a complete mess if we insert a new column within the source table. By combining VLOOKUP and MATCH as the col_index_num, we will have a dynamic and robust formula. Before we apply the MATCH formula, take a look of its syntax:

MATCH(**lookup_value**; lookup_array; [match_type])

The idea is to look the column number within the column header using match_type 0 (exact match). Thus, the formula will be like below:

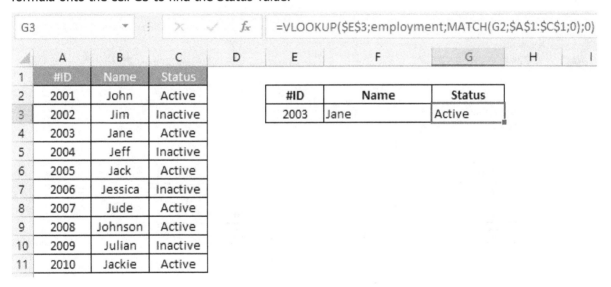

I set the cell E3 (lookup value) and range A1:C1 (lookup array) to absolute reference so that I can copy formula onto the cell G3 to find the Status value.

Define Grade Based on Score

If you want to define the grade using VLOOKUP, you must know some conditions. First, the table score must be sorted in ascending order. The other condition is that you must use TRUE argument or the formula will only look for the exact match. Take a look of example below:

⊿	A	B	C	D	E	F
1	#ID	Score	Grade			
2	3001	92				
3	3002	56				
4	3003	60				
5	3004	40			Score	Grade
6	3005	91			30	F
7	3006	45			40	E
8	3007	45			50	D
9	3008	64			60	C
10	3009	70			80	B
11	3010	93			100	A

Set the "grade" range to cell E6:F11. To find out the Grade in the column C, use formula:

=VLOOKUP(Score's Cell;Grade Range;2;1)

C2			✕ ✓ fx	=VLOOKUP(B2;grade;2;1)		

⊿	A	B	C	D	E	F	G
1	#ID	Score	Grade				
2	3001	92	B				
3	3002	56	D				
4	3003	60	C				
5	3004	40	E		Score	Grade	
6	3005	91	B		30	F	
7	3006	45	E		40	E	
8	3007	45	E		50	D	
9	3008	64	C		60	C	
10	3009	70	C		80	B	
11	3010	93	B		100	A	

VLOOKUP With Multiple Criteria

As you know, VLOOKUP only find a single criteria. However, you can manipulate it to find the multiple criteria. The concept is by adding a helper column concatenating two criteria you want to look up.

| A2 | | ▼ | : | × | ✓ | f_x | =B2&C2 |

	A	B	C	D	E
1	Helper	Name	Area	Sales	
2	JohnWest	John	West	$576,00	
3	JohnNorth	John	North	$416,00	
4	JohnEast	John	East	$570,00	
5	JohnSouth	John	South	$552,00	
6	JackWest	Jack	West	$425,00	
7	JackNorth	Jack	North	$538,00	
8	JackEast	Jack	East	$448,00	
9	JackSouth	Jack	South	$460,00	
10	JillWest	Jill	West	$566,00	
11	JillNorth	Jill	North	$418,00	
12	JillEast	Jill	East	$425,00	
13	JillSouth	Jill	South	$462,00	
14	JamesWest	James	West	$515,00	
15	JamesNorth	James	North	$578,00	
16	JamesEast	James	East	$461,00	
17	JamesSouth	James	South	$543,00	

In the picture above, a helper column is inserted to concatenate the criteria in column B and C using simple "&" formula. This column will become the lookup criteria. Thus, the VLOOKUP formula becomes as follow:

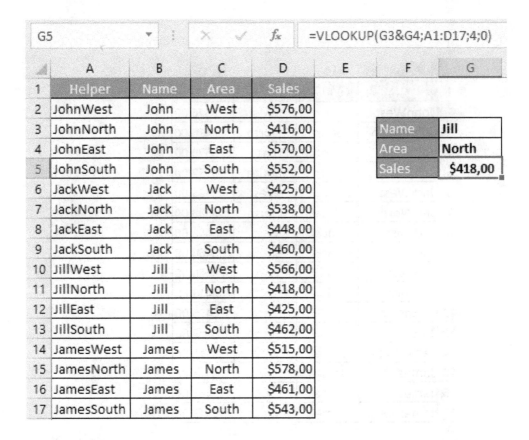

	A	B	C	D	E	F	G
	G5				f_x	=VLOOKUP(G3&G4;A1:D17;4;0)	
1	Helper	Name	Area	Sales			
2	JohnWest	John	West	$576,00			
3	JohnNorth	John	North	$416,00		Name	Jill
4	JohnEast	John	East	$570,00		Area	**North**
5	JohnSouth	John	South	$552,00		Sales	**$418,00**
6	JackWest	Jack	West	$425,00			
7	JackNorth	Jack	North	$538,00			
8	JackEast	Jack	East	$448,00			
9	JackSouth	Jack	South	$460,00			
10	JillWest	Jill	West	$566,00			
11	JillNorth	Jill	North	$418,00			
12	JillEast	Jill	East	$425,00			
13	JillSouth	Jill	South	$462,00			
14	JamesWest	James	West	$515,00			
15	JamesNorth	James	North	$578,00			
16	JamesEast	James	East	$461,00			
17	JamesSouth	James	South	$543,00			

CHARTING

"The better way to get better insight"

Chart is the best way to visualize data and get what is buried in them at a glance. The right chart can help you make the better decision. That is why you need to learn some basic charting rule to get the most of it.

Below is Excel charting tips that I find very useful and simplified:

Use simple graph like bar or line chart to get data clarity

There is nothing that can beat bar or line chart when it comes to data clarity. They are simple yet very straightforward. You can use the bar chart to see the data comparison (or ranking) rather than pie chart, and line chart to find the trend among data.

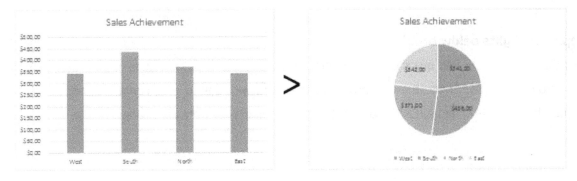

Sort the data to make it intuitive

While you are using bar chart to see the data comparison, you can get more clarity by sorting the source data so that the largest data will be on the left of the chart.

Put simple highlights below the title

Assuming that you want to find quickly the minimum, maximum, and average values of your data just by looking from the chart. Create the text boxes and fill them with link to cells containing respective formula (i.e. the MIN, MAX, and AVERAGE of data), then put them below the chart title.

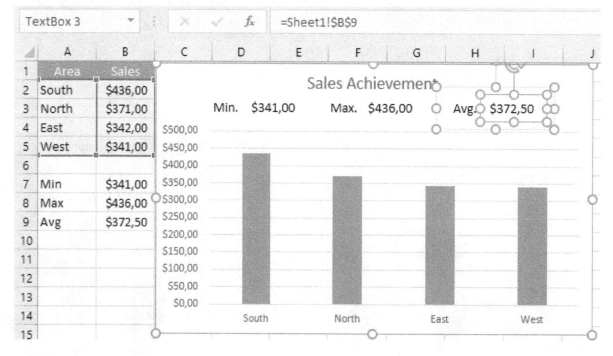

Keep the Y-Axis Simple by Shortening

You can tweak the Y-Axis without reducing its meaning to gain more space at your chart. For example, you can display million number in M instead of the actual number. Go to format axis and then change the number format using code: **\$0,, \M**

As you see in the both charts below, they are using the same source data, but chart in the right looks neat compared to the other.

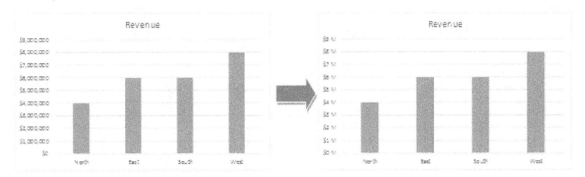

Remove the legend if it is not necessary (it occasionally be)

Legend is meant to help you identify the data representative of the chart. Somehow, the legend itself can be annoying since it can distract you. If you can identify the chart without relying on the legend, it is better to remove that annoying component.

Remove the Gridlines

Removing the gridlines can make your data on chart clearer

Paste Value Directly into Chart to Create a New Series

The following chart contains only one series of data, i.e. Mike's. To add new data series to the chart, you must click on the chart and select data from chart tools. It's quite ineffective way, though.

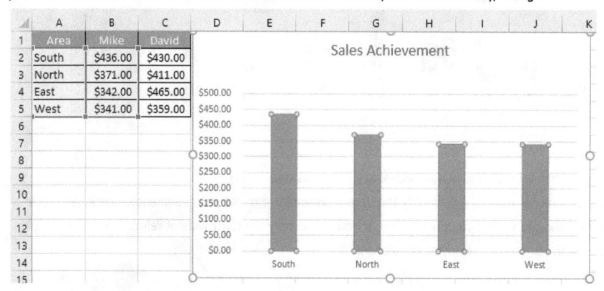

Fortunately, there is a simple way to do it. Select and copy range C2:C5, and then click on the chart, hit Ctrl+V or click paste. Voila, your chart is updated.

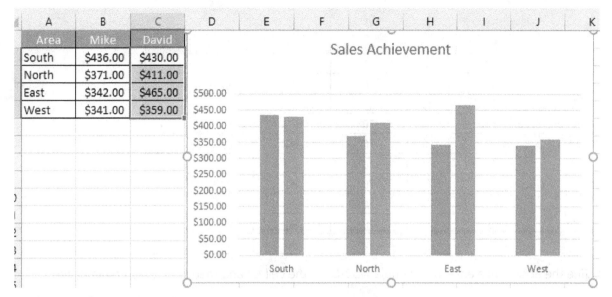

Area	Mike	David
South	$436.00	$430.00
North	$371.00	$411.00
East	$342.00	$465.00
West	$341.00	$359.00

Sales Achievement

Navigate Using Keyboard

You can make use of your keyboard to navigate inside the chart. Use the up or down arrow to move between the chart component and use left or right arrow to navigate between individual series value.

Banding Area

Chart is a great visualization tools. You can use it to view the trend of data and conclude whether it is out of trend or not. In Excel, designing the limit area is easy to do. Let's take a look of simple steps below:

We will use the data below to create a trend chart which highlights the area between lower limit and upper limit (we'll call it acceptance area). This area will be filled with color so that we will know if there is any out of limit value.

	A	B	C	D	E
1	Data	Value	Lower Limit	Upper Limit	Acceptance Area
2	1	86	70	90	
3	2	81	70	90	
4	3	88	70	90	
5	4	74	70	90	
6	5	76	70	90	
7	6	84	70	90	
8	7	78	70	90	
9	8	74	70	90	
10	9	78	70	90	
11	10	89	70	90	

To define the acceptance area, use formula =D2-C2 in the cell E2 and then copy the formula down.

E2 f_x =D2-C2

	A	B	C	D	E
1	Data	Value	Lower Limit	Upper Limit	Acceptance Area
2	1	86	70	90	20
3	2	81	70	90	20
4	3	88	70	90	20
5	4	74	70	90	20
6	5	76	70	90	20
7	6	84	70	90	20
8	7	78	70	90	20
9	8	74	70	90	20
10	9	78	70	90	20
11	10	89	70	90	20
12					

Select cell B2:B11, C2:C11, and E2:E11. Use Ctrl key to select those non contagious ranges. Go to Insert menu, and then select Stacked Column from the chart type

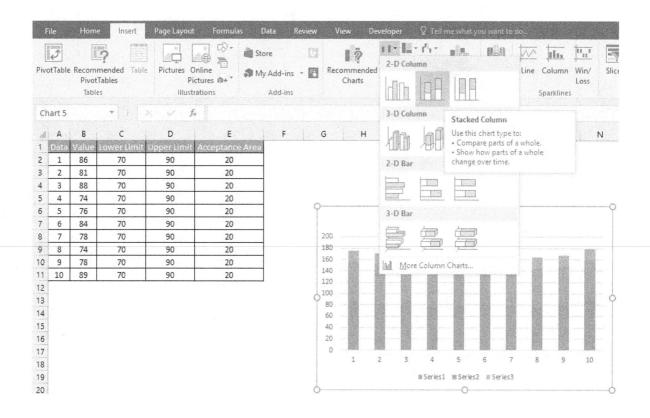

Click on the bar data that represents the value series:

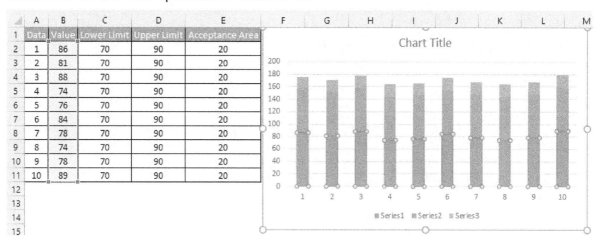

Right click on it and then select to change chart type:

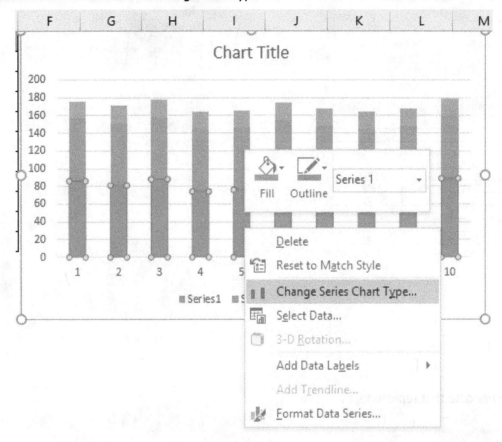

On the dialog box, select combo and then change the chart type of series 1 to Line Chart. Click OK:

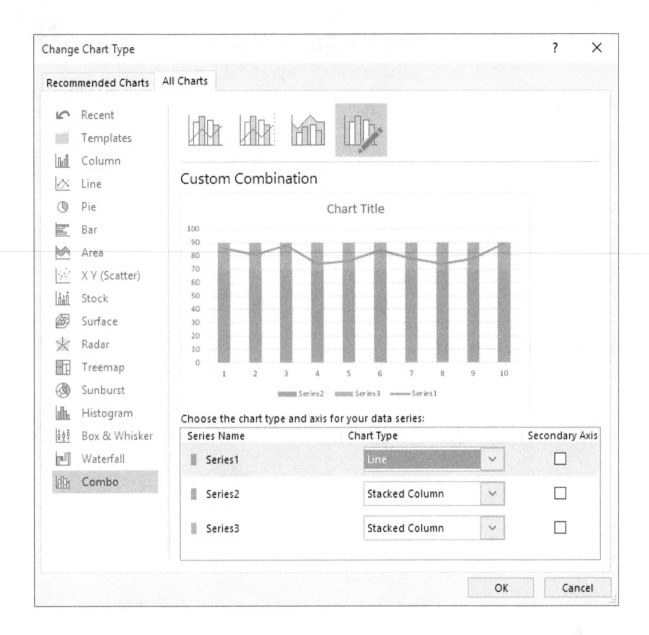

Format the bar chart by clicking on the lower series, and then set the gap width to zero:

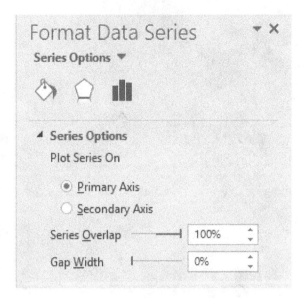

Remove the color fill by select "No fill":

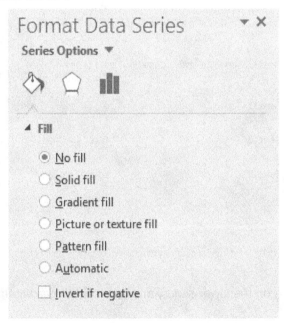

Your custom chart will look like below:

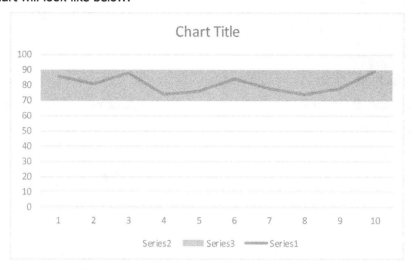

Now, let's do some cleanup. Remove the gridlines and legends. Don't forget to add the chart title:

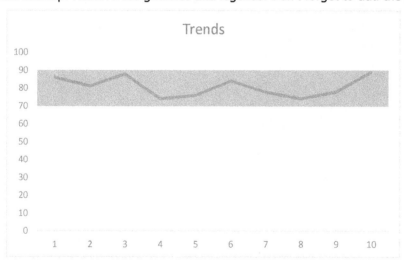

That's it. The banding area inside the chart that help you visualize the acceptance area.

VBA

"Tackle the boredom task"

VBA is Excel's powerful feature that is commonly under-utilized. Yet, it can help you getting the tedious jobs done in efficient time. It cuts the repeated action into one single command (known as macro) that you can execute, as you need it. There are two ways to setup the macro: using the macro recorder or type the code directly from Visual Basic Editor.

Macro recorder is easy to understand. It records the actions you perform and then store them into a small workbook named PERSONAL.XLSB. To use the recorded macro, you can either access it from Developer menu or hit the customized shortcut that is previously assigned during the macro recording. Before we dig into macro setup, let's make the Developer menu available onto the ribbon. If you are using Excel 2007, go to Office Button and select Excel Options. Make a tick mark on the "Show Developer tab in the Ribbon".

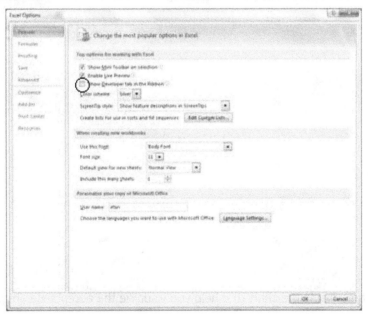

For Excel 2010 and above, the location is different. Select Customize Ribbon and then make a tick mark on the Developer tab.

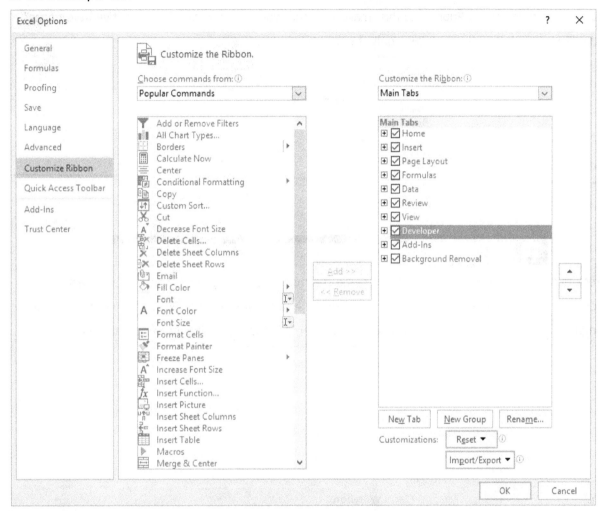

Your Developer tab will appear on the ribbon as follow:

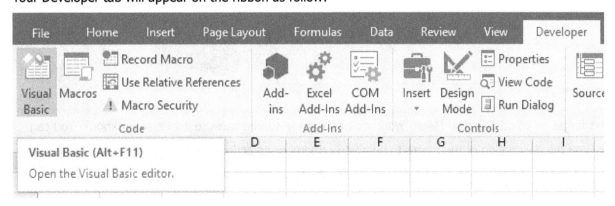

Now, let's make your first macro. As example, I want to apply Cell Style with center alignment – both vertically and horizontally. Prior to do this, make sure that you have selected "Use Relative References" on the Developer tab so that you can apply the macro at any cell.

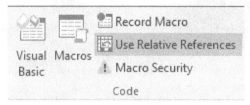

Now, click the macro recorder button:

A Record Macro box will pop out. You can name the macro and assign the shortcut key to activate it. Quick tips: combine the shortcut with Shift key as it will override the Office native shortcut (for example, you cannot use Ctrl+B to make cell content bold if it is being used for macro shortcut).

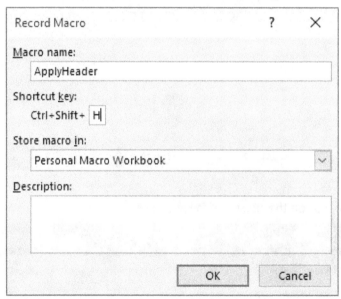

Don't forget to select Personal Macro Workbook as storage so you can use it to any workbook. You can also type the description of the macro to help you remember its action. When you are done, click OK. Now the macro is being recorded (indicated by the changing icon of the recorder):

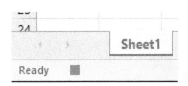

Select any cell, and then go to File, Cell Style, Accent1.

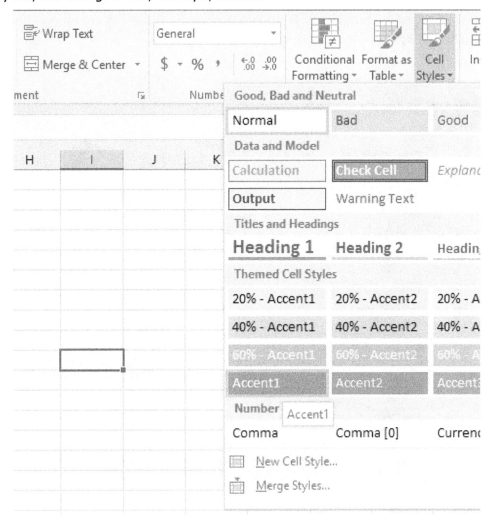

Go to Format Cells (press Ctrl+1), and then select Center for both Horizontal and Vertical Alignment. Click OK.

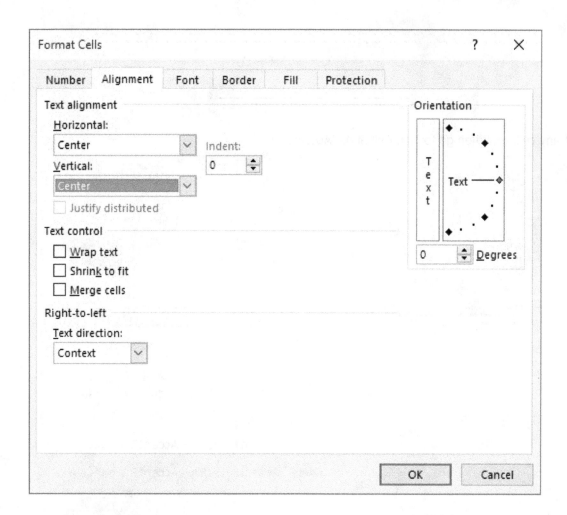

To finish the recording process, click stop recording:

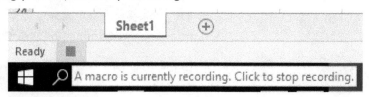

Congratulation! You just created your first macro. Now, let's try to apply it. Select the cell(s), and then press Alt+F8:

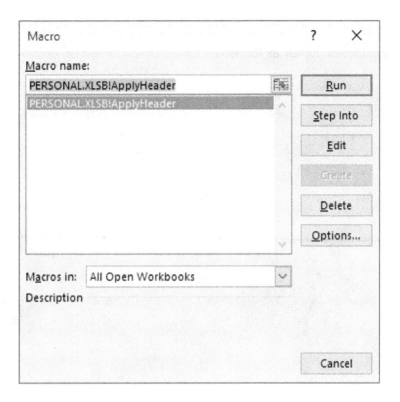

Select the macro you have just created, and then double click on it (you can also select Run or hit the shortcut key), the cells style change automatically like the picture below:

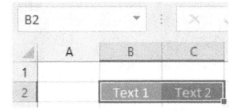

The other way to create a macro is from Visual Basic Editor, which is more flexible than macro recording as you want to take full control of the code. To launch the Visual Basic Editor, go to Developer tab and select Visual Basic or just press Alt+F11 as its shorcut.

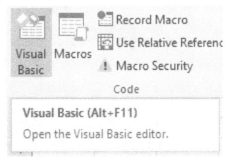

A Visual Basic Editor window will appear as follow:

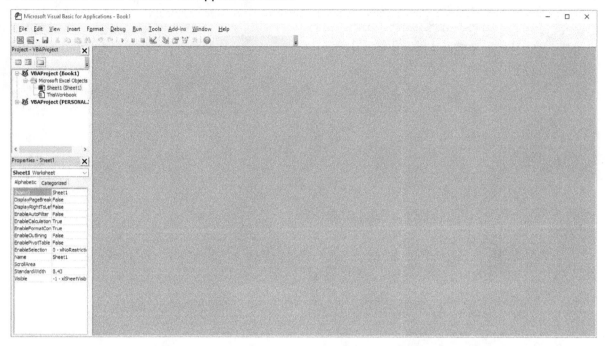

Select VBA Project (PERSONAL.XLSB), right click on it and then select Insert Module. This is where you will create a new macro.

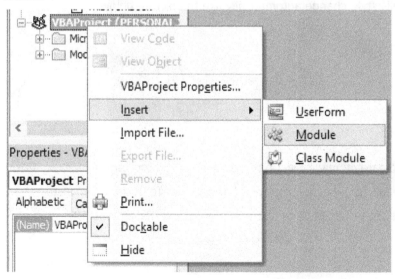

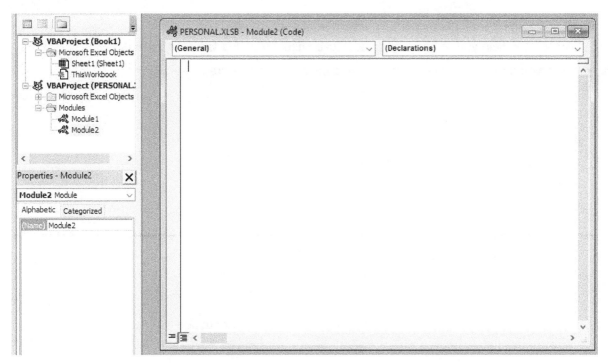

Through this chapter, I want to share some useful and handy macro modules that have helped me accomplish my tedious work in less pain and short time. Just enter the given code into each Module and see how the magic works.

Show Only Active Sheet

This VBA code will help you to show only the active sheet by hiding the other sheets. No matter how many sheets you have, they all will be hidden in a blink of an eye. Here is the code:

```
Sub ShowOnlyActiveSheet()
    Dim intSheet As Integer
    For intSheet = 1 To Sheets.Count
    If Sheets(intSheet).Name <> ActiveSheet.Name Then
    Sheets(intSheet).Visible = xlSheetHidden
    End If
    Next intSheet
End Sub
```

Copy the code above into the module and then save. Go back to Excel to see it in action.

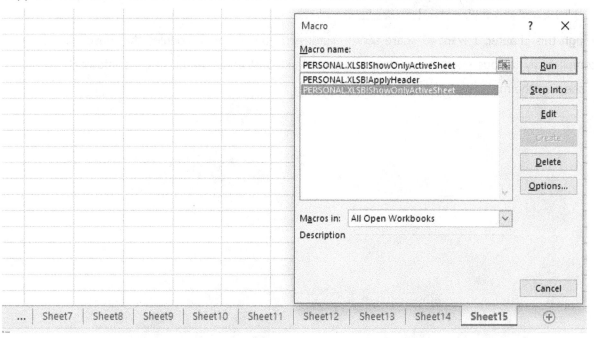

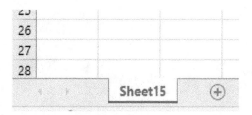

Unhide Sheets

If you hide and unhide sheets regularly, you should know that Excel couldn't unhide multiple sheets. That is why you will need this code:

```
Sub UnhideSheets()
    Dim ws As Worksheet
    For Each ws In Worksheets
    ws.Visible = xlSheetVisible
    Next ws
End Sub
```

Just like the previous code, this code will unhide all your sheets in the blink of eye:

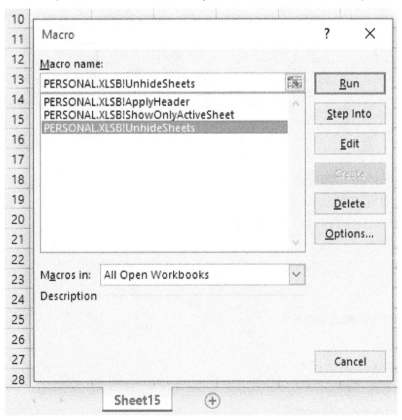

Clear the Cell's Content

This code makes the cell clearance easier. The code is easy, too:

```
Sub ClearCell()
    Selection.Clear
End Sub
```

Hide and Show Tabs

These code are extremely useful, especially if you want a strict protection to your workbook. By combining with the protect sheet, you will get fully protected workbook

```
Sub HideTabs()
    ActiveWindow.DisplayWorkbookTabs = False
End Sub
```

To show the tabs, use below code:

```
Sub ShowTabs()
    ActiveWindow.DisplayWorkbookTabs = True
End Sub
```

Insert Rows

This code makes your rows inserting easier.

```
Sub InsertRowsBelowActiveCell()
    Dim CountInsertRows As String
    CountInsertRows = InputBox( _
    "How many rows? ", _
    "Insert Rows")
    If CountInsertRows = "" Or Val(CountInsertRows) < 1 Then Exit Sub
    Rows(ActiveCell.Row + 1).Resize(Val(CountInsertRows)).Insert
End Sub
```

Activating the code will make a box pop out, waiting for your input:

	#	Data			
3			Insert Rows		×
4	1	382			
5	2	188	How many rows?		OK
6	3	449			Cancel
7	4	259			
8	5	142			
9	6	191	3		
10	7	391			

	#	Data
3		
4	1	382
5	2	188
6	3	449
7	4	259
8		
9		
10		
11	5	142
12	6	191
13	7	391

Assign Macros to Quick Access Toolbar

To use the macros, you can execute it from either Macro List or assigned shorcut. The other simple way is by adding it into the Quick Access Toolbar. Go to Customize menu from Excel Options, and then select choose Macro to be added. You can also modify the icon and description of the macros.

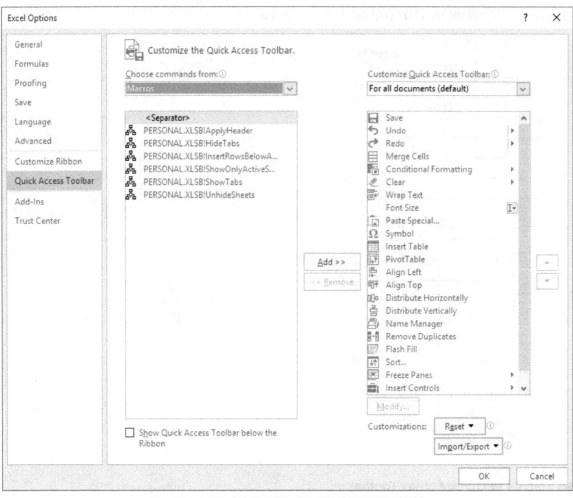

MISC. TIPS

"Additional tips that make you love Excel more"

Writing Formula efficiently

My favorite tips are using Office's built-in AutoCorrect feature. You can set it up to write formula efficiently. Here is how to do it:

- Click **File** (or Office button) →**Options**
- Select **Proofing** and then click on **AutoCorrect Options...**
- Add auto correct rules by typing the formula trigger and its replacement like this:

  vl→ =VLOOKUP

  su→ =SUM

  co → =COUNT

  etc.

Now, whenever you want to trigger the formula, just type the code above following with "**(**" and you are ready to input the formula.

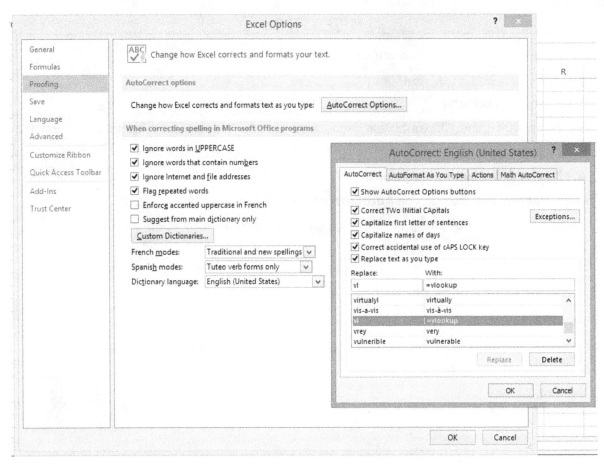

If you want to write formula which haven't listed in the autocorrect yet but you want to write it faster, you can do it by start typing the formula in the formula bar until an auto complete list appear. It will match the function you have typed so far. Select the function that you want using the keyboard or mouse then press **Tab** button to use it

Name a Range easily

By using named ranges, you can simplify your worksheet. The simplest way to name your ranged cells is typing straight from the Name Box right after you make a selection and then press Enter.

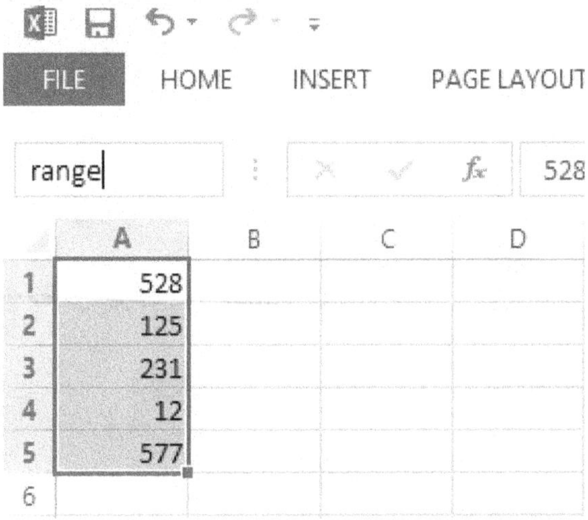

Copy Down Cell Quickly

At the first chapter, you already familiar with Ctrl+D shortcut to copy down the cell. You can use the mouse click to get the same result, too.

On the picture below, I put a simple formula to double the value from column B. To copy down the formula, move your mouse cursor to the cell's bottom-right until a fill handle appears. Double click on that fill handle.

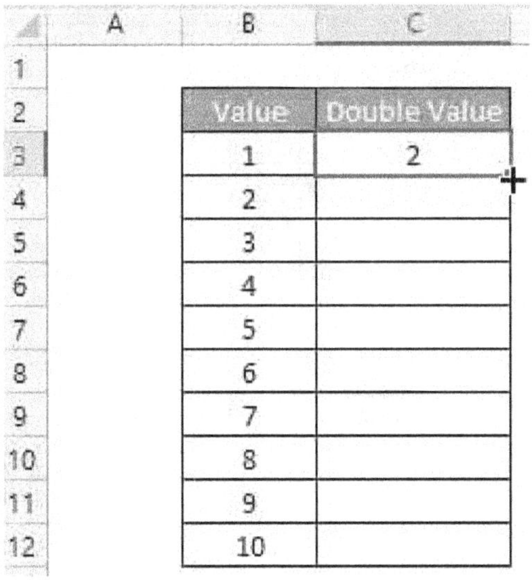

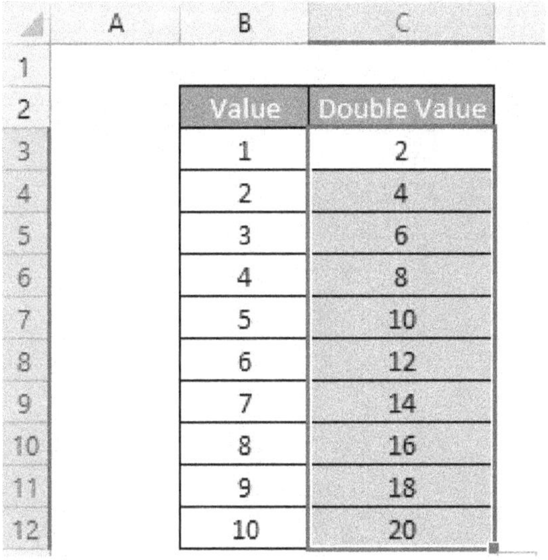

Quickly add column / row as much as you want

Assuming that you have data as shown in the picture below:

	A	B	C
1			
2	Data	Value	
3	Size	25	
4	Power	34	
5	Time	19	
6	Speed	24	
7	Resistance	33	
8	Agility	18	
9	Vitality	24	
10	Strength	27	
11	Defense	34	
12	Odds	27	
13			

After reporting those data, you are required to put additional information between Resistance and Agility, e.g. 3 additional rows. To do this, select 3 rows below Resistance (as shown in picture) and click on Insert. The same trick works well on adding column. This is more convenient than adding it one by one.

Use mouse to edit formula ranges

When you select a cell and edit the formula it contains (by pressing F2 or double-clicking the cell), you can see the colored rectangles representing the formula ranges. You can change the input by resizing these rectangles. Very handy and timesaving. It works for chart, too.

Select the ranged cells using Shift button

Instead dragging the cells to select them, you can use the helpful Shift button. Click the cell at the top-corner of selection, move your mouse cursor to the cell where the opposite bottom-corner of selection is located, then press Shift button while clicking that cell.

Click on this cell

	A	B	C	D	E	F
1						
2		x	y	z		
3		47	31	48		
4		33	38	31		
5		31	25	34		
6		31	40	25		
7		32	14	42		
8		43	22	33		
9		17	19	36		
10		10	23	44		
11						

Point the mouse to this cell, press Shift button and click the mouse

	A	B	C	D	E	F
1						
2		x	y	z		
3		47	31	48		
4		33	38	31		
5		31	25	34		
6		31	40	25		
7		32	14	42		
8		43	22	33		
9		17	19	36		
10		10	23	44		
11						

Quickly paste value-only

If you have a range of cells containing the formula and you want only the value, you can copy and then select paste special to paste the value. Fortunately, there is a quicker (and easier) to do that. Select the cells that you want to convert to value, move your mouse to the edge of your selection until the cursor changes, then use right click to drag to the next cell and move it back to current position. Release the mouse to see the paste options and select Copy Here as Values Only.

			fx	=C3*D3				
	C	D	E		F	G	H	

A	B	X
55	61	3355
45	13	585
55	20	1100
45	34	1530
93	96	8928
57	100	5700
50	100	5000

Move Here
Copy Here
Copy Here as Values Only
Copy Here as Formats Only
Link Here
Create Hyperlink Here
Shift Down and Copy
Shift Right and Copy
Shift Down and Move
Shift Right and Move
Cancel

Customize Quick Access Toolbar That Suits Your Need

It is undoubtedly that we do not use all the command in Excel. Instead, maybe there is just a few of command that we are dealing with frequently, and that's okay. The problem is, those commands are separated throughout the entire ribbon and you need to access the respective ribbon to activate it. Fortunately, there is a smarter way to occupy them all, i.e. using the Quick Access toolbar. You can customize it with your favorite commands so that you can easily access it anytime you want.

To customize it, click on the dropdown button above the ribbon then select **More Commands....** or click **File→Options** then select **Quick Access Toolbar**.

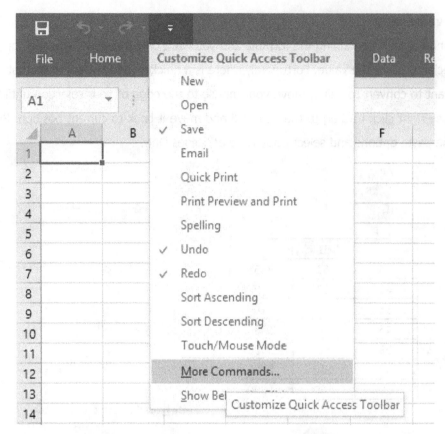

Select your favorite command then click **Add** button. When you have enough, click **OK**. Your commands will appear on Quick Access Toolbar.

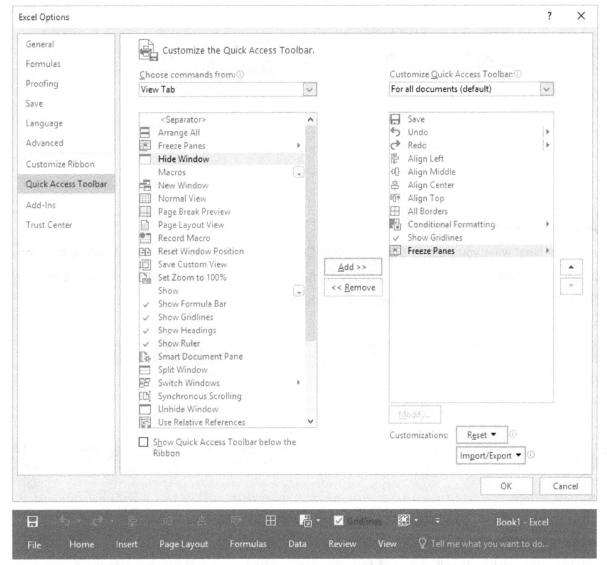

Another way (the really faster way) to add the button into Quick Access Toolbar is by highlighting the command icon and then right click to select **Add to Quick Access Toolbar** from the context menu.

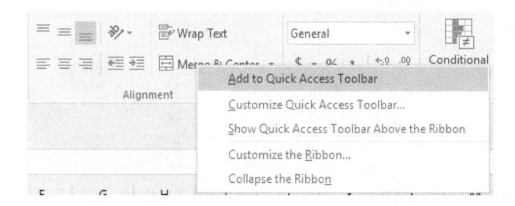

Hide That Ribbon

You already have what you need in the customized Quick Access Toolbar, so why still letting the ribbon takes some space in your work area? You can reclaim the space by double clicking one of the ribbons to make it hidden and only the ribbon name will be shown. The **Ctrl+F1** combination will do the same effect, too.

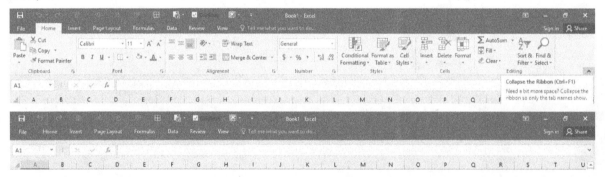

INDEX+MATCH Combo

VLOOKUP is the best answer if you want to find a data within the complex table. Unfortunately, it has one major setback, it can't go left. Therefore, instead of moving the column you are looking for to the right column, use Index + Match formula.

The Index + Match formula is the Match formula nested in the Index formula. It offers much more flexibility, speed and ease of use. The combo formula is as follows:

=INDEX(table array;**MATCH(lookup value;lookup array;[match_type])**)

To fully understand how formula combination works, look at the table below:

	A	B	C	D
1				
2		Month	Achievement	
3		January	80,00%	
4		February	83,00%	
5		March	95,00%	
6		April	86,00%	
7		May	88,00%	
8		June	90,00%	
9		July	81,00%	
10		August	87,00%	
11		September	93,00%	
12		October	84,00%	
13		November	94,00%	
14		December	82,00%	

I have a table containing the sales achievement. I name "Mnth" on the range B3:B14 and "achievement" on the range C3:C14. Let's say that I want to find which month that yield 81.00% achievement (I put this value on the Cell E3). Using the formula mention before, the combination would be like this:

=INDEX(Mnth;**MATCH(E3;achievement;0))**

And the result will be July according to the table:

F3   ▼   ⋮   ✕   ✓   *fx*   =INDEX(Mnth;MATCH(E3;achievement;0))

	A	B	C	D	E	F	G
1							
2		Month	Achievement				
3		January	80,00%		81,00%	July	
4		February	83,00%				
5		March	95,00%				
6		April	86,00%				
7		May	88,00%				
8		June	90,00%				
9		July	81,00%				
10		August	87,00%				
11		September	93,00%				
12		October	84,00%				
13		November	94,00%				
14		December	82,00%				

Double Click Sheet to Rename It

The common way to rename a sheet right clicking on it to choose Rename, which actually wastes a lot of your time. The best and simplest way is just double click on it, and you can rename it directly.

Quick Jump to the Sheet You Want

When working with multiple sheets, Excel displays only several sheet so that it will fit the sheet area next to the horizontal scroll bar. If you want to activate the sheet that is not displayed due to the capacity, you must click the triangle arrow on the left side to display the sheet you want

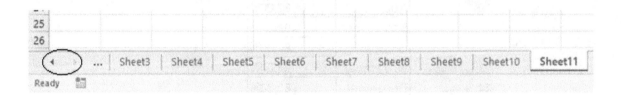

If you have many sheets to work with, that displaying process can be tedious. To make it simplified, you can right click on that triangle arrow and the pop-up window will appear containing the sheet list of the current workbook. Just select the sheet name to activate it.

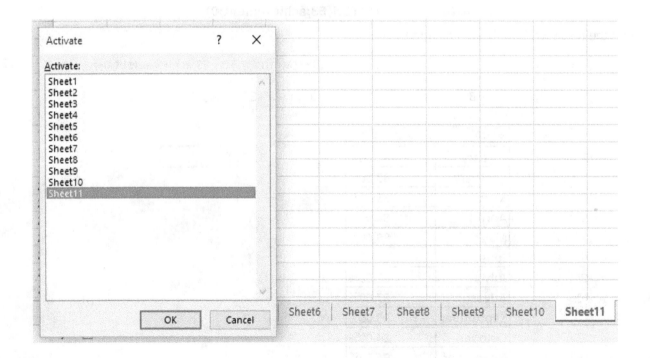

Copy the Sheet

I used to copy the sheet by using right-click and then select **Move or Copy...** from the contextual menu. If I had to repeat it for many times, it will feel inconvenient and a bit slower. Then I found this trick. Just hold the **Ctrl** key and then drag the sheet you want to copy. It's done.

Open Files in Bulk

You do not need to open files one by one if you have multiple files you need to work on. Just select the files you would like to open and then press Enter, voila! All files will open simultaneously.

Use Equal Sign (=) as Replacement for EXACT Function

The EXACT function checks whether two strings are identical, and return TRUE (if the strings are exactly the same) or FALSE (if they are not). The formula is as simple as follow:

EXACT(**text1**; text2)

Alternatively, you can use simple equal sign (=) to compare two strings and return the value like EXACT function does. The trick is just putting the equal sign between two strings you want to compare. Look at the examples below:

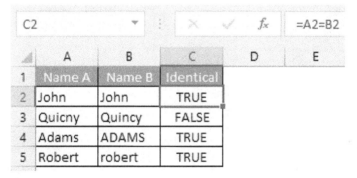

As you can see, I use the sign to compare the text value between column A and B. The formula returns to FALSE even though the text strings are similar (see Adams and Robert). This proves that the function is case sensitive, just like EXACT function.

Clear the Line Feeds

There is a time when you have cell's value like the image below and you want to transform it into a single line:

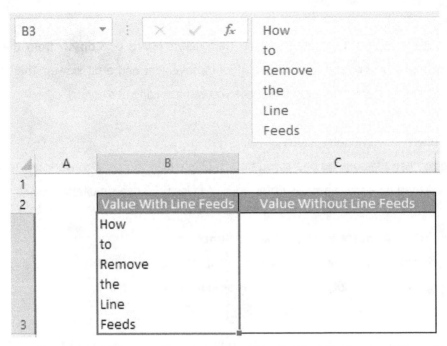

You can use several ways to get the result such as removing the line feeds manually and then replace it with the space. Or, you can use the CLEAN() function, which is simple and straight-forward:

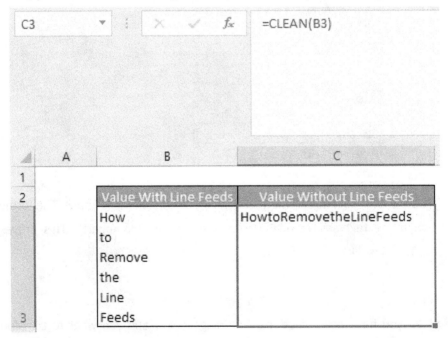

Now you can see the problem we are facing here: there is no space at all between the words.

Fortunately, there is a smarter and proper way to do it. The concept is using SUBSTITUTE() function to replace the character code of line feeds as **old_text** argument using CHAR(10) function with a space as **new_text** argument. Note that line feed character is 10 in ANSI code. Below is the formula:

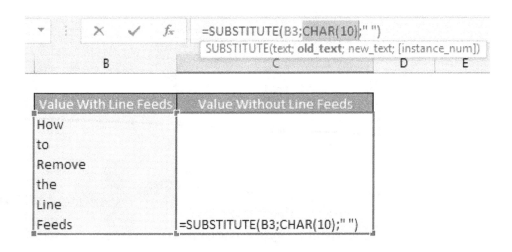

The result (clean and proper value) is as follow:

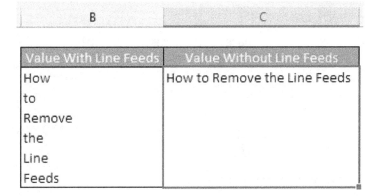

Use Space as Intersection

Now take a look again at the table below:

	A	B	C	D
1				
2		Month	Achievement	
3		January	80,00%	
4		February	83,00%	
5		March	95,00%	
6		April	86,00%	
7		May	88,00%	
8		June	90,00%	
9		July	81,00%	
10		August	87,00%	
11		September	93,00%	
12		October	84,00%	
13		November	94,00%	
14		December	82,00%	

You can use the space to find the value you want quickly. In this case, space works as intersection. This means the value we are looking for lies at the intersection of two ranges. For example, if you want to find the achievement the March, use formula:

=C3:C14 B5:C5 (The yellow highlight is a space) and the result is 95,00%

	A	B	C	D	E	F	G
1							
2		Month	Achievement				
3		January	80,00%			March	=C3:C14 B5:C5
4		February	83,00%				
5		March	95,00%	⇐			
6		April	86,00%				
7		May	88,00%				
8		June	90,00%				
9		July	81,00%				
10		August	87,00%				
11		September	93,00%				
12		October	84,00%				
13		November	94,00%				
14		December	82,00%				

Sum Value in Multiple Column Quickly

There is a shortcut to sum the value, i.e. **Alt + =**. If you assign the shortcut onto the cell below the group of value, the cell will automatically display the SUM function containing the range above it. You can also use it to sum different column respectively. Just hold Ctrl key and select each cell to place the summing value, and then press **Alt + =**.

B	C	D	E	F
20		24		38
25		35		56
13				66
22				
16				

B	C	D	E	F
20		24		38
25		35		56
13		59		66
22				160
16				
96				

Use Name Box to Select the Range

Beside its capability to name a range, you can use Name Box to make a selection of range just by typing the range you want into it. This is useful when you deal with a long range that you do not have to select and scroll the sheet to make a selection. Just type the range you want and then hit Enter.

B2:B6				B2		
	A	B			A	B
1				1		
2		45		2		45
3		42		3		42
4		44		4		44
5		41		5		41
6		40		6		40

Use Wildcards to Support the Criteria

Imagine that you want to make a report based on the following table:

	A	B	C
1	Batch	Target qty	Del. qty
2	120055	45.000	44.790
3	120035	45.000	44.660
4	120045	45.000	44.600
5	010016	45.000	44.340
6	010026	45.000	44.730
7	010036	45.000	44.540
8	010046	45.000	45.000
9	010056	45.000	44.480
10	010066	45.000	44.490
11	010076	45.000	44.800
12	010086	45.000	44.760
13	010096	45.000	44.510
14	010106	45.000	44.670
15	010116	45.000	44.700
16	010126	45.000	44.690
17	010136	45.000	44.700
18	010146	45.000	44.710
19	010156	45.000	44.730

The first two digits represent the month and the last digit represents the year. So batch 120055 means the batch manufactured in December 2015 and batch 010016 means the batch manufactured in January 2016. You are to make a report about delivered quantity made in December 2015 and January 2016. The report includes the number of batch, total, and average value. The common formula is using COUNT, SUM, AVERAGE then select the entire column C that contains batch 12...5 and 01...6 respectively. That is okay for small amount of row but will be inefficient to work with large database. This is where a wildcards help you painless. Use COUNTIF, SUMIF then add an **asterisk sign (*)** to the criteria, the formula will become like this:

	A	B	C	D	E	F	G
1	Batch	Target qty	Del. qty		Month	Result	Formula
2	120055	45.000	44.790		Dec-2015		
3	120035	45.000	44.660		Count	3	=COUNTIF(A2:A26;"12*")
4	120045	45.000	44.600		Total	134.050,00	=SUMIF(A2:A26;"12*";C2:C26)
5	010016	45.000	44.340		Average	44.683,33	=AVERAGEIF(A2:A26;"12*";C2:C26)
6	010026	45.000	44.730				
7	010036	45.000	44.540		Jan-2016		
8	010046	45.000	45.000		Count	22	=COUNTIF(A2:A26;"01*")
9	010056	45.000	44.480		Total	982650	=SUMIF(A2:A26;"01*";C2:C26)
10	010066	45.000	44.490		Average	44665,909	=AVERAGEIF(A2:A26;"01*";C2:C26)
11	010076	45.000	44.800				
12	010086	45.000	44.760				
13	010096	45.000	44.510				
14	010106	45.000	44.670				
15	010116	45.000	44.700				
16	010126	45.000	44.690				
17	010136	45.000	44.700				
18	010146	45.000	44.710				
19	010156	45.000	44.730				
20	010166	45.000	44.640				
21	010176	45.000	44.750				
22	010186	45.000	44.680				
23	010196	45.000	44.640				
24	010206	45.000	44.670				
25	010216	45.000	44.710				
26	010226	45.000	44.710				

Once you understand the concept of wildcards, you can use it for another formula that uses criteria.

www.ingramcontent.com/pod-product-compliance
Lightning Source LLC
Chambersburg PA
CBHW080544060326
40690CB00022B/5218